BATS
at Night

Kathleen A. Klatte

PowerKiDS
press
New York

Published in 2021 by The Rosen Publishing Group, Inc.
29 East 21st Street, New York, NY 10010

First Edition

Portions of this work were originally authored by Doreen Gonzales, and published as *Bats in the Dark*. All new material in this edition authored by Kathleen A. Klatte.

Editor: Kathleen Klatte
Book Design: Michael Flynn

Photo Credits: Cover (bats) Independent birds/Shutterstock.com; (series background) MoreThanPicture/Shutterstock.com; p. 4 Rudmer Zwerver/Shutterstock.com; p. 5 Liz Weber/Shutterstock.com; p. 6 Danita Delmont/Shutterstock.com; p. 7 kajornyot wildlife photography/Shutterstock.com; p.9 Ivan Kuzmin/Shutterstock.com; p. 11 riwkus/Shutterstock.com; p. 12 Martin Janca/Shutterstock.com; p 13 SNPUTHIYILLATH/Shutterstock.com; p. 15 Gucio_55/Shutterstock.com; p. 17 oNabby/Shutterstock.com; p. 18 Manuela Schewe-Behnisch/EyeEm/Getty Images; p. 19 Chanun.V/Shutterstock.com; p. 21 Yiyi Huli/Shutterstock.com; p. 22 BOONCHUAY PROMJIAM/Shutterstock.com.

Library of Congress Cataloging-in-Publication Data

Names: Klatte, Kathleen A., author.
Title: Bats at night / Kathleen A. Klatte.
Description: New York : PowerKids Press, [2021] | Series: Up all night!
   nocturnal animals | Includes index.
Identifiers: LCCN 2019045176 | ISBN 9781725318656 (paperback) | ISBN
   9781725318670 (library binding) | ISBN 9781725318663 (6 pack)
Subjects: LCSH: Bats–Juvenile literature. | Nocturnal animals–Juvenile
   literature.
Classification: LCC QL737.C5 K48 2021 | DDC 599.4–dc23
LC record available at https://lccn.loc.gov/2019045176

Some of the images in this book illustrate individuals who are models. The depictions do not imply actual situations or events.

Manufactured in the United States of America

CPSIA Compliance Information: Batch #CSPK20. For Further Information contact Rosen Publishing, New York, New York at 1-800-237-9932.

CONTENTS

THAT'S NOT A BIRD!. 4

BIG BATS AND LITTLE BATS 6

NIGHT WINGS!. 8

WHICH WAY TO THE BAT CAVE? 10

IN-FLIGHT MEALS 12

SOUNDS LIKE DINNER!. 14

ROOST, SWEET ROOST 16

BABY BATS. 18

IT WAS A DARK AND STORMY NIGHT. 20

BATS ARE OUR FRIENDS 22

GLOSSARY 23

INDEX. 24

WEBSITES 24

THAT'S NOT A BIRD!

What animal flies around at night but isn't a bird? It might be a bat! Bats are **nocturnal** animals that fly around at night looking for food. At sunrise, they return to their homes to hang upside down and sleep.

Bats are the only **mammals** that fly. They have small bodies and long, wide wings. A nocturnal life is good for bats. Many kinds of bats eat **insects** that fly around at night. Night feeding also keeps bats safe from animals that might eat them. Cooler air temperatures at night help protect bats from overheating when they fly.

THIS LITTLE BROWN BAT IS HANGING AROUND AND WAITING FOR THE SUN TO GO DOWN. HIS WINGS ARE TUCKED IN, AND HIS FUR BLENDS WITH THE BARK OF THE TREE HE'S HANGING ON.

BIG BATS AND LITTLE BATS

Scientists recognize more than 1,200 different species, or kinds, of bats. These bats are separated into two main groups: megabats and microbats. "Micro" means "very small." Most microbats range from 1.5 to 6 inches (3.8 to 15.2 cm) long. Microbats use echoes to find food in the darkness. They're found all over the world.

THE LESSER LONG-NOSED BAT EATS THE FRUIT AND NECTAR OF CACTI THAT BLOOM AT NIGHT. ITS BODY IS ONLY ABOUT 3 INCHES (7.6 CM) LONG.

"Mega" means "huge." Even though a few megabats are small, many of these mammals are large. For example, flying foxes have wings as wide as 5 feet (1.5 m) from tip to tip! Megabats use sight and smell to find food. Some bats have better vision than people do.

WHILE YOU'RE SLEEPING

Bats belong to the **order** Chiroptera, which means "hand wing" in Greek. They got this name because they have four long fingers and a thumblike claw that are connected by flesh to form the wing.

7

NIGHT WINGS!

A bat's wings are much larger than its body. A bat's body is covered in brown, black, gray, yellow, or red fur. Some may have fur that's striped or **mottled**.

Different species of bats have differently shaped wings and different styles of flying. They've adapted to their **environment** and the type of food they eat. Bats that hunt can fly very quickly. Bats that eat nectar have wings better suited to hovering.

Bats have a claw that sticks out of each wing. It's about where a thumb would be located. They can use this claw to walk or to move food to their mouth.

A BAT'S FINGER BONES ARE LOCATED INSIDE ITS WINGS. THESE BONES ARE VERY FLEXIBLE, OR EASILY MOVABLE, AND BATS CAN SHIFT THEM INSIDE THEIR WINGS WHEN THEY FLY.

9

WHICH WAY TO THE BAT CAVE?

Bats are found almost everywhere in the world. Some bats live in rain forests, while others live in deserts. Wherever they live, bats roost in dark, out-of-the-way places during the day. Bats like to roost in caves, rocky places, and trees. They also live under bridges and in barns.

When bats find somewhere safe to roost, they take hold with their claws and hang with their heads pointing down. Then, they fold their wings around their body and go to sleep. Bats sleep upside down. Some types of bats will creep along the ceiling of their roost by moving one toe at a time!

WHILE YOU'RE SLEEPING

Some bats can take flight by flapping their wings like birds. Most must fall into flight. This is one reason why they hang upside down.

BUILDING A BAT HOUSE IS A GREAT WAY TO BRING BATS TO YOUR YARD. THE BATS WILL HAPPILY EAT MANY OF THE BUGS THAT BOTHER PEOPLE, AND THEY MIGHT EVEN HELP **POLLINATE** YOUR FLOWERS!

11

IN-FLIGHT MEALS

Bats eat all sorts of things. Most microbats are insectivores. This means these bats eat insects, such as moths and crickets. Bats catch small insects in their mouth. They catch large insects with their wings and then pull them into their mouth. Bats can eat as many as 1,000 insects every hour!

BATS THAT FEED ON FRUIT AND NECTAR ARE IMPORTANT TO THEIR ENVIRONMENT. THEY HELP POLLINATE FLOWERS AS THEY FEED, AND THEIR DROPPINGS MOVE SEEDS AROUND TO GROW NEW PLANTS.

Some microbats eat small animals such as birds, lizards, and frogs. Some even catch and eat fish. Many megabats eat fruit or the nectar of flowers. Vampire bats eat the most surprising food. These bats bite animals and lick the blood from the bite. Vampire bats usually don't take enough blood to hurt the animals they feed from.

SOUNDS LIKE DINNER!

Different types of bats use different senses to locate food. Because they're active at night, it's too dark to see much around them. Bats tend to use other methods to find their dinner. For example, megabats use smell along with sight to find food.

Microbats hunt with sound. They make beeping noises as they fly. They listen for a beep to echo off something in their path. Bats use this echo to figure out where an object is. The echo also tells the bat how large the object is, which direction it's moving in, and how fast it's moving. This is called echolocation. It's a very good way to hunt flying targets.

WHILE YOU'RE SLEEPING

Contrary to what you might have heard, bats aren't blind. Megabats seem to have very good night vision. Microbats tend to depend more on their other senses.

A BAT'S EARS TEND TO BE QUITE LARGE COMPARED TO THE SIZE OF ITS BODY. HEARING IS A VERY IMPORTANT SENSE FOR ANIMALS THAT HUNT AT NIGHT.

ROOST, SWEET ROOST

Most bats live in groups called colonies. Bat colonies can have thousands of bats. Bats in colonies take care of each other and even bring food to bats that are sick. In some cases, bats do live alone.

Bats that live where the weather gets cold can't find food in the winter. Many of these bats **hibernate**. Hibernating bats find a roost and hang there, upside down. In time, their bodies cool down and their breathing slows. By hibernating, bats can live through times when there is little food. Other bats from cold places **migrate** to warm places when winter comes. Bats often return to the same seasonal roosts each year.

A GROUP OF BATS FLYING IS SOMETIMES CALLED A "CLOUD." LOOKING AT THIS PHOTO, IT'S VERY EASY TO SEE HOW THAT NAME CAME ABOUT!

BABY BATS

Bats are mammals, so they give birth to live young. A baby bat is called a pup. Most bats have one pup at a time. Some species of bats migrate to special nursery roosts to give birth and raise their young.

A pup drinks its mother's milk. Mother bats sometimes carry their new pups with them when they go out to feed.

THIS BAT PUP IS HANGING AROUND WITH ITS MOTHER. WHEN THE MOTHER TAKES FLIGHT, THE PUP WILL HANG ON WITH CLAWS AND MAYBE EVEN TEETH.

A baby bat is about a quarter of its mother's size. It has little to no hair and is sometimes blind and deaf at birth. Bat pups grow quickly. Mother bats teach their babies how to fly just a few weeks after birth.

WHILE YOU'RE SLEEPING

Everyone has seen pictures of bats sleeping or eating while hanging upside down, but did you know that mother bats also give birth that way?

19

IT WAS A DARK AND STORMY NIGHT

There are lots of myths and stories about bats. One famous story tells of bats turning into vampires at night. Vampires are monsters who suck people's blood in stories. Though people know vampires aren't real, some people are still afraid of bats.

People sometimes worry that bats will fly into their hair. Others fear a bat will bite them and make them sick. However, bats generally stay away from people and don't often bite them. Like many other mammals, though, bats can carry **rabies**. It's always best to leave wild animals alone.

BATS MEAN HAPPINESS AND GOOD FORTUNE IN CHINESE FOLKLORE. THEY'VE BEEN SHOWN IN ALL SORTS OF ARTWORK FOR CENTURIES.

BATS ARE OUR FRIENDS

Like every other creature on Earth, bats have an important part to play. Some kinds of bats eat insects that can make people sick or destroy crops. Other types of bats help plants by spreading their seeds.

Today, though, bats are in danger. People keep moving into places where bats live. This leaves the bats without a home. Several kinds of bats, such as the bumblebee bat, the Mariana flying fox, and the Ozark big-eared bat, are even in danger of dying out. Luckily, people have started finding ways to keep bats and their homes safe. The more that people learn about bats, the safer their future will be.